GOD OF CARNAGE

BY
YASMINA REZA

TRANSLATED BY
CHRISTOPHER HAMPTON

★

★

DRAMATISTS
PLAY SERVICE
INC.

NOTE ON BILLING

Anyone receiving permission to produce GOD OF CARNAGE is required to give credit to Yasmina Reza and Christopher Hampton as sole and exclusive Author and Translator of the Play on the title page of all programs distributed in connection with performances of the Play and in all instances in which the title of the Play appears for purposes of advertising, publicizing or otherwise exploiting the Play and/or a production thereof. The names of the Author and Translator must appear as shown below on separate lines, in which no other names appear, immediately beneath the title and in size of type equal to 50% of the size of the largest, most prominent letter used for the title of the Play. No person, firm or entity may receive credit larger or more prominent than that accorded the Author and Translator.

GOD OF CARNAGE
by Yasmina Reza
Translated by Christopher Hampton

In addition, the following acknowledgment must appear on the title page in all programs distributed in connection with performances of the Play, and in all advertising and publicity in which full production credits appear:

GOD OF CARNAGE was produced on Broadway by
Robert Fox, David Pugh & Dafydd Rogers, Stuart Thompson,
Scott Rudin, Jon B. Platt, The Weinstein Company,
and The Shubert Organization.

SPECIAL NOTE ON SONGS/RECORDINGS

Dramatists Play Service neither holds the rights to nor grants permission to use any songs or recordings mentioned in the Play. Permission for performances of copyrighted songs, arrangements or recordings mentioned in this Play is not included in our license agreement. The permission of the copyright owner(s) must be obtained for any such use. For any songs and/or recordings mentioned in the Play, other songs, arrangements, or recordings may be substituted provided permission from the copyright owner(s) of such songs, arrangements or recordings is obtained; or songs, arrangements or recordings in the public domain may be substituted.

GOD OF CARNAGE received its Broadway premiere at the Bernard Jacobs Theatre on March 22, 2009. It was directed by Matthew Warchus; the set and costume design were by Mark Thompson; the lighting design was by Hugh Vanstone; the sound design was by Simon Baker and Chris Cronin; and the music was by Gary Yershon. The cast was as follows:

ALAN .... Jeff Daniels
ANNETTE .... Hope Davis
MICHAEL .... James Gandolfini
VERONICA .... Marcia Gay Harden

CHARACTERS

ALAN RALEIGH

ANNETTE RALEIGH

MICHAEL NOVAK

VERONICA NOVAK

All in their forties.
A living room.
No realism.
Nothing superfluous.

.

GOD OF CARNAGE

The Novaks and the Raleighs, sitting down, facing one another. We need to sense right away that the place belongs to the Novaks and that the two couples have just met. In the center, a coffee table, covered with art books. Two big bunches of tulips in vases. The prevailing mood is serious, friendly and tolerant.

VERONICA. So, this is our statement … You'll be doing your own, of course … At 5:30 P.M. on the third of November, in Cobble Hill Park, following a verbal altercation, Benjamin Raleigh, eleven, armed with a stick, struck our son Henry Novak in the face. This action resulted in, apart from a swelling of the upper lip, the breaking of two incisors, including injury to the nerve in the right incisor.

ALAN. Armed?

VERONICA. Armed? You don't like armed, what shall we say, Michael, furnished, equipped, furnished with a stick, is that all right?

ALAN. Furnished, yes.

MICHAEL. Furnished with a stick.

VERONICA. *(Making the correction.)* Furnished. The irony is, we've always regarded Cobble Hill Park as a haven of security, unlike Whitman Park.

MICHAEL. She's right. We've always said, Cobble Hill Park yes, Whitman Park no.

VERONICA. Absolutely. Anyway, thank you for coming. There's nothing to be gained from getting stuck down some emotional cul-de-sac.

ANNETTE. We should be thanking you. We should.

VERONICA. I don't see that any thanks are necessary. Fortunately, there is still such a thing as the art of co-existence, isn't there?

ALAN. Which the children don't appear to have mastered. At least, not ours!

ANNETTE. Yes, not ours! … What's going to happen to the tooth with the affected nerve? …

VERONICA. We don't know yet. They're being cautious about the prognosis. Apparently the nerve hasn't been totally exposed.

MICHAEL. Only a little bit of it's been exposed.

VERONICA. Yes. Some of it's been exposed and some of it's still covered. That's why they've decided not to kill the nerve just yet.

MICHAEL. They're trying to give the tooth a chance.

VERONICA. Obviously it would be best to avoid endodontic surgery.

ANNETTE. Well, yes …

VERONICA. So there'll be an interim period while they give the nerve a chance to recover.

MICHAEL. In the meantime, they'll be giving him ceramic crowns.

VERONICA. Whatever happens, you can't have an implant before you're eighteen.

MICHAEL. No.

VERONICA. Permanent implants can't be fitted until you finish growing.

ANNETTE. Of course. I hope … I hope it all works out.

VERONICA. Yes, I hope so. *(Slight pause.)*

ANNETTE. Those tulips are gorgeous.

VERONICA. They're from that little Korean deli up on Smith Street. You know, the one at the end.

ANNETTE. Oh, yes.

VERONICA. They come every morning direct from Holland, forty dollars for a bunch of fifty.

ANNETTE. Oh, really!

VERONICA. You know, the one at the end.

ANNETTE. Yes, yes.

VERONICA. You know he didn't want to identify Benjamin.

MICHAEL. No, he didn't.

VERONICA. Impressive sight, that child, face bashed in, teeth missing, still refusing to talk.

ANNETTE. I can imagine.

MICHAEL. He also didn't want to identify him for fear of looking like a tattletale in front of his friends, we have to be honest, Veronica, it was nothing more than bravado.

VERONICA. Of course, but bravado is a kind of courage, isn't it?

ANNETTE. That's right ... So how...? What I mean is how did you manage to get Benjamin's name? ...

VERONICA. Well, we explained to Henry he wasn't helping this child by shielding him.

MICHAEL. We said to him if this child thinks he can keep on hitting people with impunity, why should he stop?

VERONICA. We said to him if we were this kid's parents, we would definitely want to be told.

ANNETTE. Absolutely.

ALAN. Yes ... *(His cell phone vibrates.)* Excuse me ... *(He moves away from the group; as he talks, he pulls a newspaper out of his pocket.)* Yes, Murray, thanks for calling back. Right, in today's *Times*, let me read it to you ... According to a paper published in the *Lancet* and taken up yesterday in the *Financial Times*, two Australian researchers have revealed the neurological side effects of Antril, a hypertensive beta-blocker, manufactured at the Verenz-Pharma laboratories. These side effects range from hearing loss to ataxia ... So who the hell is your media watchdog ... Yes, it's very goddamn inconvenient ... No, what's most inconvenient about it as far as I'm concerned is the annual shareholders' meeting's in two weeks. Do you have an insurance contingency to cover litigation? ... OK ... Oh, and Murray, Murray, ask your PR gal to find out if this story shows up anywhere else ... Call me back. *(He hangs up.)* ... Excuse me.

MICHAEL. So you're ...

ALAN. A lawyer.

ANNETTE. What about you?

MICHAEL. Me, I have a wholesale company, household goods; and Veronica's a writer and works part-time in an art history bookshop.

ANNETTE. A writer?

VERONICA. I contributed to a collection on the civilization of Sheba, based on the excavations that were restarted at the end of the Ethiopian-Eritrean war. And I have a book coming out in January on the Darfur tragedy.

ANNETTE. So you specialize in Africa.

VERONICA. I'm very interested in that part of the world.

ANNETTE. Do you have any other children?

VERONICA. Henry has a nine-year-old sister, Camille. Who's furious at her father because last night her father got rid of the hamster.

ANNETTE. You got rid of the hamster?

MICHAEL. Yes. This hamster makes the most godawful racket all night, then spends the whole day fast asleep! Henry was in a lot of pain last night; he was being driven crazy by the noise that the hamster was making. And, to tell you the truth, I've been wanting to get rid of it for a long time, so I said to myself, OK, that's it, I took it and put it in the street. I thought they loved drains and gutters and all that, but I guess not, it just sat there paralyzed on the sidewalk. Well, they're not domestic animals, they're not wild animals, I don't really know where their natural habitat is. Dump them in the woods, they're probably just as unhappy, so I don't know where you're supposed to put them.

ANNETTE. You left it outside?

VERONICA. He left it there and tried to convince Camille it had run away. But she wasn't having it.

ALAN. Was the hamster gone this morning?

MICHAEL. Gone, yes.

VERONICA. And you, what field are you in?

ANNETTE. I'm in wealth management.

VERONICA. Is it at all possible … forgive me for putting the question so bluntly, that Benjamin might apologize to Henry?

ALAN. It'd be good if they talked.

ANNETTE. He has to apologize, Alan. He has to tell him he's sorry.

ALAN. Yes, yes. Of course.

VERONICA. But is he sorry?

ALAN. He realizes what he's done. He just doesn't understand the implications. He's eleven.

VERONICA. If you're eleven, you're not a baby any more.

MICHAEL. You're not an adult either! We haven't offered you anything, coffee, tea, is there any of that clafouti left, Ronnie? It's an extraordinary clafouti!

ALAN. I wouldn't mind an espresso.

ANNETTE. Just some water.

MICHAEL. *(To Veronica, on her way out.)* Espresso for me too, sweetie, and bring the clafouti anyway. *(After a hiatus.)* What I always say is, we're a lump of potter's clay and it's up to us to fashion something out of it. Perhaps it won't take shape till the very end. Who knows?

ANNETTE. Mm.

MICHAEL. You have to taste this clafouti. Good clafouti is an endangered species.

ANNETTE. You're right.

ALAN. What is it you sell?

MICHAEL. Domestic hardware. Locks, doorknobs, soldering irons, all sorts of household goods, saucepans, frying pans ...

ALAN. Money in that, is there?

MICHAEL. Well, you know, it's never exactly been a bonanza, it was pretty hard when we started. But if I'm out there every day pushing my product, we survive. At least it's not seasonal, like textiles. Although we do sell a lot of fondue pots around Christmastime!

ALAN. I'm sure ...

ANNETTE. When you saw the hamster sitting there, paralyzed, why didn't you bring it back home?

MICHAEL. Because I couldn't pick it up.

ANNETTE. You put it on the sidewalk.

MICHAEL. I took it out in its cage and sort of tipped it out. I don't like to touch rodents. *(Veronica comes back with a tray. Drinks and the clafouti.)*

VERONICA. I don't know who put the clafouti in the fridge. Monica puts everything in the fridge, she won't be told. What's Benjamin said to you? Sugar?

ALAN. No, thanks. What's in the clafouti?

VERONICA. Apples and pears.

ANNETTE. Apples and pears?

VERONICA. My own little recipe. *(She cuts the clafouti and distributes slices.)* It's going to be too cold, it's a shame.

ANNETTE. Apples and pears, this is a first.

VERONICA. Apples and pears, it's pretty textbook, but there's a little trick to it.

ANNETTE. There is?

VERONICA. Pears need to be cut thicker than apples. Because pears cook faster than apples.

ANNETTE. Ah, of course.

MICHAEL. But wait, she's not telling you the real secret.

VERONICA. Let them try it.

ALAN. Very good. It's very good.

ANNETTE. Tasty.

VERONICA. ... Gingerbread crumbs!

ANNETTE. Brilliant!

VERONICA. To be quite honest, I got it from his mother.

ALAN. Gingerbread, delicious ... Well, at least all this has given us a new recipe.

VERONICA. I'd have preferred it if it hadn't cost my son two teeth.

ALAN. Of course, that's what I meant.

ANNETTE. Strange way of expressing it.

ALAN. Not at all, I ... *(His cell phone vibrates, he looks at the screen.)* I have to take this ... Yes, Murray ... No, no, don't ask for right of reply, you'll only feed the controversy ... Are you insured? ... Mm, mm ... What are these symptoms, what is ataxia? ... What about on a standard dose? ... How long have you known about this? ... And all that time you never recalled it? ... What's the gross? ... Ah, got it. I see ... *(He hangs up and immediately dials another number, scarfing clafouti all the while.)*

ANNETTE. Alan, do you mind joining us?

ALAN. Yes, yes, I'm coming ... *(To the cell.)* Serge? ... They've known about the risks for two years ... An internal report, but it didn't formally identify any undesirable side effects ... No, they took no precautions, they didn't insure, not a word about it in the annual report ... Impaired motor skills, stability problems, in short you look completely retarded ... *(He laughs along with his colleague.)* They are grossing one hundred and fifty million dollars ... Blanket denial ... Idiot wanted to demand a right of reply. We certainly don't want a right of reply, on the other hand if the story spreads we could put out a press release, say it's disinformation leaked two weeks before the shareholders' meeting ... He's going to call me back ... OK. *(He hangs up.)* I haven't had lunch.

MICHAEL. Please, help yourself, help yourself.

ALAN. Thanks. I have no manners. What were we saying?

VERONICA. That it would have been nicer to meet under different circumstances.

ALAN. Oh, yes, right. So the clafouti, it's your mother's?

MICHAEL. The recipe is my mother's, but Ronnie made this one.

VERONICA. Your mother doesn't mix pears and apples!

MICHAEL. No.

VERONICA. Poor thing has to have an operation.

ANNETTE. Really? What for?

VERONICA. Her knee.

MICHAEL. They're going to insert a rotatable prosthesis made of metal and polyethylene. She's wondering what's going to be left of it when she's cremated.

VERONICA. Don't be horrible.

MICHAEL. She refuses to be buried next to my father. She wants to be cremated and put next to her mother who's all on her own in Florida. Two urns, looking out to sea, trying to get a word in edgewise. Ha, ha! … *(Smiles all round. Pause.)*

ANNETTE. We're very touched by your generosity. We appreciate the fact you're trying to calm the situation down rather than exacerbate it.

VERONICA. Frankly, it's the least we can do.

MICHAEL. Yes!

ANNETTE. Not at all. How many parents standing up for their children become infantile themselves? If Henry had broken two of Benjamin's teeth, I'm afraid Alan and I would have been a lot more thin-skinned about it. I'm not certain we'd have been so broad-minded.

MICHAEL. Of course you would!

ALAN. She's right. Not at all certain.

MICHAEL. Oh, yes. Because we all know it could easily have been the other way around. *(Pause.)*

VERONICA. So what does Benjamin have to say about it? How does he view the situation?

ANNETTE. He's not saying much. I think he's still slightly in shock.

VERONICA. He understands that he's disfigured his playmate?

ALAN. No. No, he does not understand that he's disfigured his playmate.

ANNETTE. Why are you saying that? Benjamin understands very well!

ALAN. He understands he's behaved like a thug, he does not understand that he's disfigured his playmate.

VERONICA. You don't care for the word, but the word is unfortunately accurate.

ALAN. My son has not disfigured your son.

VERONICA. Your son has disfigured my son. Come back at five and have a look at his mouth and teeth.

MICHAEL. Temporarily disfigured.

ALAN. The swelling on his lip will go down, and as for his teeth, take him to the best dentist, I'm prepared to chip in …

MICHAEL. That's what the insurance is for. What we'd like is for the boys to make up so that this sort of thing never happens again.

ANNETTE. Let's arrange a meeting.

MICHAEL. Yes. That's the answer.

VERONICA. Should we be there?

ALAN. They don't need to be coached. Just let them do it man to man.

ANNETTE. Man to man, Alan, don't be ridiculous. Having said that, we don't necessarily have to be there. It'd probably be better if we weren't, wouldn't it?

VERONICA. The question isn't whether we should be there or not. The question is do they want to talk to one another, do they want to have a discussion?

MICHAEL. Henry wants to.

VERONICA. What about Benjamin?

ANNETTE. It's no use asking his opinion.

VERONICA. But it has to come from him.

ANNETTE. Benjamin has behaved like a hooligan, we're not interested in what mood he's in.

VERONICA. If Benjamin is forced to meet Henry in a punitive context, I can't see the results would be very positive.

ALAN. Madam, our son is a savage. To hope for any kind of spontaneous repentance would be fanciful. Right, I'm sorry, I have to get back to the office. You stay, Annette, you'll tell me what you've decided, I'm no use whichever way you cut it. Women always think you need a man, you need a father, as if they'd be any help at all. Men are a dead weight, they're clumsy and maladjusted, oh, you can see the F train, that's great!

ANNETTE. I'm so embarrassed, but I can't stay either … My husband has never exactly been a stroller dad! …

VERONICA. What a pity. It's lovely, taking the baby for a walk. And it lasts such a short time. You always enjoyed taking care of the children, didn't you, Michael, you loved pushing the stroller.

MICHAEL. Yes, I did.

VERONICA. So what have we decided?

ANNETTE. Could you come by the house with Henry about seven-thirty?

VERONICA. Seven-thirty? … What do you think, Michael?

MICHAEL. Well … Honestly …

ANNETTE. Go on.

MICHAEL. I think Benjamin ought to come here.

VERONICA. Yes, I agree.

MICHAEL. I don't think it's right for the victim to go traipsing around.

VERONICA. That's right.

ALAN. Personally, I can't be anywhere at seven-thirty.

ANNETTE. Since you're no use, we won't be needing you.

VERONICA. All the same, it would be better if his father were here. *(Alan's cell phone vibrates.)*

ALAN. All right, but then it can't be this evening … Yeah? … There's no mention of this in the executive report. And no risk has been formally established. There's no evidence … *(He hangs up.)*

VERONICA. Tomorrow?

ALAN. I'm flying to The Hague tomorrow.

VERONICA. You're working in The Hague?

ALAN. I have a case at the International Criminal Court.

ANNETTE. The main thing is that the children speak to one another. I'll bring Benjamin here at seven-thirty and we can leave them to have their discussion. No? You don't look very convinced.

VERONICA. If Benjamin is not made aware of his responsibilities, they'll just look at each other like a pair of china dogs, it'll be a catastrophe.

ALAN. What do you mean? What do you mean, made aware of his responsibilities?

VERONICA. I'm sure your son is not a savage.

ANNETTE. Of course Benjamin isn't a savage.

ALAN. Yes he is.

ANNETTE. Alan, this is absurd, why say something like that?

ALAN. He's a savage.

MICHAEL. How does he explain his behavior?

ANNETTE. He doesn't want to discuss it.

VERONICA. But he ought to discuss it.

ALAN. He ought to do any number of things. He ought to come here, he ought to discuss it, he ought to be sorry for it, clearly you have parenting skills that put us to shame, we hope to improve, but in the meantime, please bear with us.

MICHAEL. All right! This is idiotic. Let's not end up like this!

VERONICA. I'm only thinking of him, I'm only thinking of Benjamin.

ALAN. I got the message.

ANNETTE. Let's just sit down for another couple of minutes.

MICHAEL. A little more coffee?

ALAN. A coffee, okay.

ANNETTE. Then I'll have one too. Thanks.

MICHAEL. That's all right, Ronnie, I'll do it. *(Pause. Annette delicately shuffles some of the numerous art books dispersed around the coffee table.)*
ANNETTE. I see you're a great art lover.
VERONICA. Art. Photographs. To some extent it's my job.
ANNETTE. I adore Bacon.
VERONICA. Ah, yes, Bacon.
ANNETTE. *(Turning the pages.)* … Cruelty. Majesty.
VERONICA. Chaos. Balance.
ANNETTE. That's right …
VERONICA. Is Benjamin interested in art?
ANNETTE. Not as much as he should be … What about your children?
VERONICA. We try. We try to fill the gaps in the education system.
ANNETTE. Yes …
VERONICA. We try to make them read. To take them to concerts and exhibits. We're eccentric enough to believe in the soothing powers of culture!
ANNETTE. And you're right … *(Michael comes back with the coffee.)*
MICHAEL. So, clafouti, is it a cake or a tart? Serious question. I was just thinking in the kitchen, Linzertorte, for example, is that a tart? Come on, come on, you can't leave that one little slice.
VERONICA. Clafouti is a cake. The pastry's not rolled out, it's mixed in with the fruit.
ALAN. You really are a cook.
VERONICA. I love it. The thing about cooking is you have to love it. In my opinion, it's only the classic tart, that's to say on a pastry base, that deserves to be called a tart.
MICHAEL. What about you, do you have other children?
ALAN. A son from my first marriage.
MICHAEL. I was wondering, not that it's at all important, what started the fight. Henry won't say one single word about it.
ANNETTE. Henry refused to let Benjamin join his gang.
VERONICA. Henry has a gang?
ALAN. He also called Benjamin a snitch.
VERONICA. Did you know Henry had a gang?
MICHAEL. No. That's terrific!
VERONICA. Why is it terrific?
MICHAEL. Because I had my own gang.
ALAN. Me too.

14

VERONICA. And what does that entail?

MICHAEL. There are five or six kids that follow you and are ready to sacrifice themselves. Like in *Spartacus*.

ALAN. Absolutely, like in *Spartacus*!

VERONICA. Who knows about *Spartacus* these days?

ALAN. They use a different model. Spiderman.

VERONICA. Anyway, clearly you know more than we do. Benjamin hasn't been as silent as you implied. And do we know why Henry called him a snitch? No, sorry, stupid, that's a stupid question. First of all, I couldn't care less, also, it's beside the point.

ANNETTE. We can't get involved in children's quarrels.

VERONICA. And it's none of our business.

ANNETTE. No.

VERONICA. On the other hand, what is our business is what unfortunately happened. The violence, that's our business.

MICHAEL. To become the head of my gang, when I was twelve, I had to fight Bobby Kopecki, who was bigger than me, one-on-one, single combat.

VERONICA. What are you talking about, Michael? What's that got to do with it?

MICHAEL. No, you're right, it's got nothing to do with it.

VERONICA. We're not discussing single combat. The children weren't fighting.

MICHAEL. I know, I know. I just suddenly had a flashback.

ALAN. There's not that big a difference.

VERONICA. Oh, yes, there is. Excuse me, there's a very big difference.

MICHAEL. There's a very big difference.

ALAN. What?

MICHAEL. With Bobby Kopecki, we'd agreed to have a fight.

ALAN. Did you beat the shit out of him?

MICHAEL. Up to a point.

VERONICA. Alright, can we forget Bobby Kopecki? Would you allow me to speak to Benjamin?

ANNETTE. By all means!

VERONICA. I wouldn't want to do it without your permission.

ANNETTE. Speak to him. What could be more natural?

ALAN. Good luck.

ANNETTE. Stop it, Alan. I don't understand you.

ALAN. Mrs. Novak …

VERONICA. Veronica. We don't have to be so formal.

ALAN. Veronica, you're motivated by an educational impulse, which is very sympathetic …

VERONICA. If you don't want me to speak to him, I won't speak to him.

ALAN. No, speak to him, read him the riot act, do what you like.

VERONICA. I don't understand why you don't seem to care about this.

ALAN. Ma'am …

MICHAEL. Veronica.

ALAN. Of course I care, Veronica, enormously. My son has injured another child …

VERONICA. On purpose.

ALAN. See, that's the kind of remark that gets my back up. Obviously, on purpose.

VERONICA. But that makes all the difference.

ALAN. The difference between what and what? That's what we're talking about. Our son picked up a stick and hit your son. That's why we're here, isn't it?

ANNETTE. This is pointless.

MICHAEL. Yes, she's right, this kind of argument is pointless.

ALAN. Why do you feel the need to slide in on purpose? What kind of message is that supposed to be sending me?

ANNETTE. Listen, we're on a slippery slope, my husband is desperate about all kinds of other things, I'll come back this evening with Benjamin and we'll let things sort themselves out naturally.

ALAN. I'm not in the least bit desperate.

ANNETTE. Well, I am.

MICHAEL. There's nothing to be desperate about.

ANNETTE. Yes, there is. *(Alan's cell phone vibrates.)*

ALAN. … Don't make any statement … No comment … No, of course you can't take it off the market! If you take it off the market, you become responsible … The minute you take Antril off the market, you're admitting liability! There's nothing in the annual accounts. If you want to be sued for falsifying the executive report and get shitcanned in two weeks, take it off the market …

VERONICA. Last year, on Parents' Day, wasn't it Benjamin who was in that play…?

ANNETTE. *Charley's Aunt.*

VERONICA. *Charley's Aunt.*

ALAN. We'll think about the victims later, Murray ... let's see what the shares do after the annual meeting ...

VERONICA. He was extraordinary.

ANNETTE. Yes ...

ALAN. We are not going to take the medicine off the market just because two or three people are bumping into the furniture! ... Don't make any statements for the time being ... Yes. I'll call you back ... *(He cuts him off and phones his colleague.)*

VERONICA. I remember him very clearly in *Charley's Aunt.* Do you remember him, Michael?

MICHAEL. Yes, yes ...

VERONICA. He was hilarious when he was in drag.

ANNETTE. Yes ...

ALAN. *(To his colleague.)* ... They're panicking, they've got the media up their ass, you have to prepare a press release, not something defensive, not at all, on the contrary, go out all guns blazing, you insist that Verenz-Pharma is the victim of a destabilization attempt two weeks before its annual shareholders' meeting, where does this paper come from, why did it have to fall out of the sky right now, et cetera and so on ... Don't say anything about health problems, just ask one question: Who's behind this report? ... Right. *(He hangs up. Brief pause.)*

MICHAEL. They're terrible, these pharmaceutical companies. Profit, profit, profit.

ALAN. You're not supposed to be listening to my conversation.

MICHAEL. You're not obliged to have it in front of me.

ALAN. Yes, I am. I'm absolutely obliged to have it here. Not my choice, believe me.

MICHAEL. They dump any old crap on you without giving it a second thought.

ALAN. In the therapeutic field, every advance brings with it risk as well as benefit.

MICHAEL. Yes, I understand that. All the same. Funny job you have.

ALAN. Meaning?

VERONICA. Michael, this has nothing to do with us.

MICHAEL. Funny job.

ALAN. And what is it you do?

MICHAEL. I have an ordinary job.

ALAN. What is an ordinary job?

MICHAEL. I told you, I sell frying pans.

ALAN. And doorknobs.

MICHAEL. And toilet fittings. Lots of other things.

ALAN. Ah, toilet fittings. Now we're talking. That's really interesting.

ANNETTE. Alan.

ALAN. It's really interesting. I'm interested in toilet fittings.

MICHAEL. Why shouldn't you be?

ALAN. How many types are there?

MICHAEL. Two different systems. Gravity or pressure-assist.

ALAN. I see.

MICHAEL. Depending on the feed.

ALAN. Well, yes.

MICHAEL. Either the water comes down from above or up from below.

ALAN. Yes.

MICHAEL. I could introduce you to one of my stock managers who specializes in this kind of thing, if you like. You'd have to leg it out to Secaucus, though.

ALAN. You seem to be very on top of the subject.

VERONICA. Are you intending to punish Benjamin in any way? You can carry on with the plumbing in some more appropriate setting.

ANNETTE. I'm not feeling well.

VERONICA. What's the matter?

ALAN. Yes, you're very pale, sweetheart.

MICHAEL. A little pale, certainly.

ANNETTE. I feel nauseous.

VERONICA. Nauseous? … I have some Pepto-Bismol …

ANNETTE. No, no … It'll be all right …

VERONICA. What could we…? Coke. Coke's very good. *(She immediately sets off in search of it.)*

ANNETTE. I'll be all right …

MICHAEL. Walk around a little. Take a few steps. *(She takes a few steps. Veronica comes back with the Coca-Cola.)*

ANNETTE. Really? You think so? …

VERONICA. Yes, yes. Small sips.

ANNETTE. Thank you … *(Alan has discreetly called his office.)*

ALAN. … Give me Serge, will you please? … Oh, right … Ask him to call me back, ask him to call me back right away … *(He hangs up.)* Is it good, Coca-Cola? I thought it was just supposed to be for diarrhea.

VERONICA. Not only for that. *(To Annette.)* Alright?

ANNETTE. Alright … Veronica, if we want to reprimand our child, we'll do it in our own way and without having to account to anybody.

MICHAEL. Absolutely.

VERONICA. What do you mean, absolutely, Michael?

MICHAEL. They can do whatever they want with their son, it's their prerogative.

VERONICA. I don't think so.

MICHAEL. What do you mean you don't think so, Ronnie?

VERONICA. I don't think it is their prerogative.

ALAN. Really? Explain. *(His cell phone vibrates.)* I'm sorry … *(To his colleague.)* Excellent … But don't forget, nothing's been proved, there's nothing definite … Get this straight, if anyone fucks up, Murray is a dead man in two weeks, and us with him.

ANNETTE. That's enough, Alan! That's enough now with the cell phone! Will you pay attention to what's going on here, shit!

ALAN. Yes … Call me back and read it to me. *(He hangs up.)* What's the matter with you, have you gone nuts, shouting like that? Serge heard everything.

ANNETTE. Good! Drives me crazy, that cell phone, endlessly!

ALAN. Listen, Annette, I'm already doing you a big favor by being here in the first place …

VERONICA. Extraordinary thing to say.

ANNETTE. I'm going to throw up.

ALAN. No, you're not, you are not going to throw up.

ANNETTE. Yes, I am …

MICHAEL. Would you like to use the bathroom?

ANNETTE. *(To Alan.)* No one's forcing you to stay.

VERONICA. No, no one's forcing him to stay.

ANNETTE. I'm feeling dizzy …

ALAN. Stare at a fixed point. Stare at a fixed point, Woof-woof.

ANNETTE. Go away, leave me alone.

VERONICA. She would be better off in the bathroom.

ALAN. Go to the bathroom. Go to the bathroom if you want to throw up.

MICHAEL. Give her some Pepto-Bismol.

ALAN. You don't suppose it could be the clafouti?

VERONICA. It was made yesterday!

ANNETTE. *(To Alan.)* Don't touch me! …

ALAN. Calm down, Woof-woof.

MICHAEL. Please, let's not get worked up about nothing.

ANNETTE. According to my husband, everything to do with house, school or garden is my department.

ALAN. No, it's not!

ANNETTE. Yes, it is. And I understand why. It's deathly, all of it. It's deathly.

VERONICA. If you think it's so deathly, why have children in the first place?

MICHAEL. Maybe Benjamin senses your lack of interest.

ANNETTE. What lack of interest?

MICHAEL. You just said … *(Annette vomits violently. A brutal and catastrophic spray, part of which goes over Alan. The art books on the coffee table are likewise deluged.)* Go get the dishpan, go get the dishpan! *(Veronica runs out to look for a pan and Michael hands her the coffee tray, just in case. Annette retches again, but nothing comes out.)*

ALAN. You should have gone to the bathroom, Woof-woof, this is ridiculous!

MICHAEL. Looks like your suit ate most of it! *(Very soon, Veronica is back with a basin and a cloth. The basin is given to Annette.)*

VERONICA. Well, it's absolutely not the clafouti, couldn't possibly be.

MICHAEL. It's not the clafouti, it's nerves. This is pure nerves.

VERONICA. *(To Alan.)* Would you like to clean up in the restroom? Oh, no, the Kokoschka! Oh, my God! *(Annette vomits bile into the basin.)*

MICHAEL. Give her some Pepto-Bismol.

VERONICA. Not now, she can't keep anything down.

ALAN. Where's the restroom?

VERONICA. I'll show you. *(Veronica and Alan leave.)*

MICHAEL. It's nerves. It's a panic attack. You're a mom, Annette. Whether you want to be or not. I understand why you feel desperate.

ANNETTE. Mmm.

MICHAEL. What I always say is, you can't control the things that control you.

ANNETTE. Mmm …

MICHAEL. With me, it's the cervical vertebrae. The vertebrae seize up.

ANNETTE. Mmm … *(She brings up a little more bile. Veronica returns with another basin, containing a sponge.)*

VERONICA. What are we going to do about the Kokoschka?

MICHAEL. Well, I would spray it with Mr. Clean … the problem is how to dry it … Or else you could sponge it down and put a bit of perfume on it.

VERONICA. Perfume?

MICHAEL. Use my Kouros, I never wear it.

VERONICA. It'll warp.

MICHAEL. We could run the hair dryer over it and flatten it out under a pile of other books. Or iron it, like they do with money.

VERONICA. Oh, my God …

ANNETTE. I'll buy you another one.

VERONICA. You can't find it! It went out of print years ago!

ANNETTE. I'm so sorry …

MICHAEL. We'll salvage it. Let me do it, Ronnie. *(She hands him the basin of water and the sponge, disgusted. Michael gets started on cleaning up the book.)*

VERONICA. It's a reprint of the catalogue from the '53 London exhibition, more than twenty years old! …

MICHAEL. Go get the hair dryer. And the Kouros. In the linen closet.

VERONICA. Her husband's in the restroom.

MICHAEL. Well, he's not naked, is he? *(She goes out as he continues to clean up.)* … There, that's the worst of it. *The People of the Tundra* needs a bit more of a wipe … I'll be back. *(He goes out with the used basin. Veronica and Michael return more or less simultaneously. She has the bottle of perfume, he has the basin containing fresh water. Michael finishes cleaning up.)*

VERONICA. *(To Annette.)* Feeling better?

ANNETTE. Yes …

VERONICA. Can we spray now?

MICHAEL. Where's the hair dryer?

VERONICA. He's bringing it when he's finished with it.

MICHAEL. We'll wait for him. We'll put the Kouros on last thing.

ANNETTE. Can I use the bathroom as well?

VERONICA. Yes. Yes, yes. Of course.

ANNETTE. I can't tell you how sorry I am … *(Veronica takes her out and returns immediately.)*

VERONICA. What a nightmare! Horrible!

MICHAEL. Tell you what, he'd better not push me any further.

VERONICA. She's dreadful as well.

MICHAEL. Not as bad.

VERONICA. She's a phony.

MICHAEL. Less irritating.

VERONICA. They're both dreadful! Why do you keep siding with them? *(She sprays the tulips.)*

MICHAEL. I don't keep siding with them, what are you talking about?

VERONICA. You keep vacillating, trying to play both ends against the middle.

MICHAEL. No, I don't!

VERONICA. Yes, you do. Going on about your triumphs as a gang leader, telling them they're free to do whatever they like with their son when the child is a public menace; when a child's a public menace, it's everybody's concern, I can't believe she puked all over my books! *(She sprays the Kokoschka.)*

MICHAEL. *(Pointing.)* Put some on *The People of the Tundra* …

VERONICA. If you think you're about to hurl, you go to the proper place.

MICHAEL. … And the Foujita.

VERONICA. *(Spraying everything.)* This is disgusting.

MICHAEL. I was pushing it a little bit with the shithouse systems.

VERONICA. You were brilliant.

MICHAEL. Good answers, don't you think?

VERONICA. Brilliant. The stock manager thing was brilliant.

MICHAEL. What an asshole. And what did he call her?! …

VERONICA. Woof-woof.

MICHAEL. That's right, Woof-woof!

VERONICA. Woof-woof! *(They both laugh. Alan returns, hair dryer in hand.)*

ALAN. That's right, I call her Woof-woof.

VERONICA. Oh … I'm sorry, I didn't mean to be rude … It's so easy to make fun of other people's nicknames! What about us, what do we call each other, Michael? Far worse, isn't it?

ALAN. Did you want the hair dryer?

VERONICA. Thank you.

MICHAEL. Thank you. *(He takes the hair dryer.)* We call each other Darjeeling, like the tea. That's more ridiculous, if you ask me! *(Michael switches on the machine and starts drying the books. Veronica flattens out the damp pages.)* Smooth them out, smooth them out.

VERONICA. *(As she smoothes out the pages, raising her voice above the noise.)* How's the poor thing feeling, better?

ALAN. Better.

VERONICA. I reacted very badly, I'm ashamed of myself.

ALAN. Not at all.

VERONICA. I just steam-rollered her about my catalogue, I can't believe I did that.

MICHAEL. Turn the page. Stretch it out, stretch it out all the way.

ALAN. You're going to tear it.

VERONICA. You're right … He's right, Michael. That's enough, Michael, it's dry. Objects can become ridiculously important, half the time you can't even remember why. *(Michael shuts the catalogue and they both cover it with a little cairn of heavy books. Michael finishes drying the Foujita,* The People of the Tundra, *etc. …)*

MICHAEL. There we are! Good as new. Where does Woof-woof come from?

ALAN. How much is that doggie in the window.

MICHAEL. I know it! I know the one! *(He hums.)* Woof-woof! Ha, ha! … Ours comes from our honeymoon in India. It's idiotic, really!

VERONICA. Shouldn't I go and see how she is?

MICHAEL. Off you go, Darjeeling.

VERONICA. Shall I? … *(Annette returns.)* Ah, Annette! I was worried about you … Are you feeling better?

ANNETTE. I think so.

ALAN. If you're not sure, stay away from the coffee table.

ANNETTE. I left the towel in the bathtub, I wasn't sure where to put it.

VERONICA. Perfect.

ANNETTE. You've cleaned it all up. I'm so sorry.

MICHAEL. Everything's great. Everything's in order.

VERONICA. Annette, forgive me, I've hardly paid any attention to you. I've been obsessed with my Kokoschka.

ANNETTE. Don't worry about it.

VERONICA. The way I reacted, very bad of me.

ANNETTE. Not at all … *(After an embarrassed pause.)* Something occurred to me in the bathroom …

VERONICA. Yes?

ANNETTE. Perhaps we skated too hastily over … I mean, what I mean is …

MICHAEL. Say it, Annette, say it.

ANNETTE. An insult is also a kind of assault.

MICHAEL. Of course it is.

VERONICA. Well, that depends, Michael.

MICHAEL. Yes, it depends.

ANNETTE. Benjamin's never shown any signs of violence. He wouldn't have done that without a reason.

ALAN. He got called a snitch! *(His cell phone vibrates.)* … I'm sorry! … *(He moves to one side, making elaborately apologetic signs to Annette.)* Yes … As long as there aren't any statements from victims. We don't want any victims. I don't want you being quoted alongside victims! … A blanket denial and if necessary attack the newspaper … They'll fax you the draft of the press release, Murray. *(He hangs up.)* If anyone calls me a snitch, I'm liable to get annoyed.

MICHAEL. Unless it's true.

ALAN. What did you say?

MICHAEL. I mean, suppose it's justified?

ANNETTE. My son is a snitch?

MICHAEL. 'Course not, I was joking.

ANNETTE. Yours is as well, if that's how it's going to be.

MICHAEL. What do you mean, ours is as well?

ANNETTE. Well, he did identify Benjamin.

MICHAEL. Because we insisted!

VERONICA. Michael, this is completely beside the point.

ANNETTE. What's the difference? Whether you insisted or not, he gave you the name.

ALAN. Annette.

ANNETTE. Annette what? *(To Michael.)* You think my son is a snitch?

MICHAEL. I don't think anything.

ANNETTE. Well, if you don't think anything, don't say anything. Stop making these insinuations.

VERONICA. Let's stay calm, Annette. Michael and I are making an effort to be reasonable and moderate …

ANNETTE. Not that moderate.

VERONICA. Oh, really? What do you mean?

ANNETTE. Moderate on the surface.

ALAN. I really have to go, Woof-woof …

ANNETTE. All right, go on, be a coward.

ALAN. Annette, right now I'm risking my most important client, so this responsible parent routine …

VERONICA. My son has lost two teeth. Two incisors.

ALAN. Yes, yes, I think we all got that.

VERONICA. One of them for good.

ALAN. He'll have new ones, we'll give him new ones! Better ones! It's not as if he's burst an eardrum!

ANNETTE. We're making a mistake not to take into account the origin of the problem.

VERONICA. There's no origin. There's just an eleven-year-old child hitting someone. With a stick.

ALAN. Armed with a stick.

MICHAEL. We withdrew that word.

ALAN. You withdrew it because we objected to it.

MICHAEL. We withdrew it without any protest.

ALAN. A word deliberately designed to rule out error or clumsiness, to rule out childhood.

VERONICA. I'm not sure I'm able to take much more of this tone of voice.

ALAN. You and I have had trouble seeing eye-to-eye right from the start.

VERONICA. There's nothing more infuriating than to be attacked for something you yourself consider a mistake. The word armed was inappropriate, so we changed it. Although, if you stick to the strict definition of the word, its use is far from inaccurate.

ANNETTE. Benjamin was insulted and he reacted. If I'm attacked, I defend myself, especially if I find myself alone, confronted by a gang.

MICHAEL. Puking seems to have perked you up.

ANNETTE. Do you have any idea how crude that sounds?

MICHAEL. We all mean well. All four of us, I'm sure. Why let these minor irritants, these pointless aggravations push us over the edge? …

VERONICA. Oh, Michael, that's enough! Let's stop beating around the bush. If all we are is moderate on the surface, let's forget it.

MICHAEL. No, no, I refuse to allow myself to slide down that slope.

ALAN. What slope?

MICHAEL. The shitty slope those two little bastards have perched us on! There, I've said it!

ALAN. I'm not sure Ronnie has quite the same outlook.

VERONICA. Veronica!

ALAN. Sorry.

VERONICA. So now Henry's a little bastard, is he? That is the last straw!

ALAN. Right, well, I really do have to go.

ANNETTE. Me too.

VERONICA. Go on, go, I give up. *(The telephone rings.)*

MICHAEL. Hello? … Oh, Mom … No, no, we're with some friends, but tell me about it … do whatever the doctor wants you to do … They've given you Antril?! Wait a minute, Mom, wait a minute, don't go away … *(To Alan.)* Antril's your crap, isn't it? My mother's taking it!

ALAN. Thousands of people take it.

MICHAEL. You stop taking that stuff right now. Do you hear what I'm saying, Mom? Immediately … Don't argue, I'll explain later … Tell Dr. Perolo I'm forbidding you to take it … Why glow-in-the-dark? … That's completely ridiculous … All right, we'll talk about it later. Lots of love, Mom. I'll call you back. *(He hangs up.)* … She's rented glow-in-the-dark crutches, so she doesn't get knocked down by a truck. As if someone in her condition would be strolling down the BQE in the middle of the night. They've given her Antril for her blood pressure.

ALAN. If she takes it and stays normal, I'll have her called as a witness. Didn't I have a scarf? Ah, there it is.

MICHAEL. I don't appreciate your cynicism. If my mother displays the most minor symptom, I'll be starting a class action.

ALAN. Oh, that'll happen anyway.

MICHAEL. Well, I would hope so.

ANNETTE. Goodbye, Mr. and Mrs. Novak.

VERONICA. Behaving well gets you nowhere. Courtesy is a waste of time, it weakens you and undermines you …

ALAN. Right, come on, Annette, let's go, enough preaching and sermons for today.

MICHAEL. Go on, go. But can I say one thing? Having met you two, it's pretty clear that for what's-his-name, Benjamin, there are mitigating circumstances.

ANNETTE. When you murdered that hamster …

MICHAEL. Murdered?!

ANNETTE. Yes.

MICHAEL. I murdered the hamster?!

ANNETTE. Yes. You've done your best to make us feel guilty, but your virtue went straight out the window once you decided to be a killer.

MICHAEL. I absolutely did not murder that hamster!

ANNETTE. Worse. You left it, shivering with terror, in a hostile environment. That poor hamster is bound to have been eaten by a dog or a rat.

VERONICA. It's true! That is true!

MICHAEL. What do you mean, that is true!

VERONICA. It's true. What do you expect me to say? It's appalling what must have happened to that creature.

MICHAEL. I thought the hamster would be happy to be liberated. I thought it was going to run off down the gutter, jumping for joy!

VERONICA. Well, it didn't.

ANNETTE. And you abandoned it.

MICHAEL. I can't touch those things! For fuck's sake, Ronnie, you know very well, I'm incapable of touching that whole species!

VERONICA. He has a phobia about rodents.

MICHAEL. That's right, I'm frightened of rodents, I'm terrified of snakes, anything close to the ground, I don't want them near me. So that's the end of it!

ALAN. *(To Veronica.)* And you, why didn't you go out and look for it?

VERONICA. Because I had no idea what had happened! Michael didn't tell us, me and the children, that the hamster had escaped, till the following morning. I went out immediately, immediately, I walked around the block, I even went down to the basement.

MICHAEL. Veronica, I find it intolerable to be on trial all of a sudden for this hamster saga that you've seen fit to reveal. It's a personal matter which is nobody else's business but ours and which has nothing to do with the present situation! And I find it incomprehensible to be called a killer! In my own home!

VERONICA. What's your home got to do with it?

MICHAEL. My home, the doors of which I have opened, the doors of which I have opened wide in a spirit of reconciliation, to people who ought to be grateful to me for it!

ALAN. It's wonderful the way you keep patting yourself on the back.

ANNETTE. Don't you feel any guilt?

MICHAEL. I feel no guilt whatsoever. I've always found that creature repulsive. I'm ecstatic that it's gone.

VERONICA. Michael, that's ridiculous.

MICHAEL. What's ridiculous? Have you gone crazy as well? Their son beats up Henry, and I get shit on because of a hamster?

VERONICA. You behaved very badly with that hamster, you can't deny it.

MICHAEL. Fuck the hamster!

VERONICA. You won't be able to say that to your daughter this evening.

MICHAEL. Bring her on! I'm not going to let myself be told how to behave by some nine-year-old snot-nose.

ALAN. Hundred per cent behind you there.

VERONICA. Pathetic.

MICHAEL. Careful, Veronica, you be careful, I've been extremely restrained up to now, but I'm two inches away from crossing that line.

ANNETTE. And what about Henry?

MICHAEL. What about Henry?

ANNETTE. Isn't he upset?

MICHAEL. If you remember, Henry has other problems.

VERONICA. Henry was less attached to Nibbles.

MICHAEL. Stupid name as well!

ANNETTE. If you feel no guilt, why do you expect our son to feel any?

MICHAEL. Let me tell you something, I'm up to here with these idiotic discussions. We tried to be nice, we bought tulips, my wife passed me off as a liberal, but I can't keep this bullshit up any more. I am not a member of polite society. What I am and always have been, is a fucking Neanderthal.

ALAN. Aren't we all?

VERONICA. No. No. I'm sorry, we are not all fucking Neanderthals.

ALAN. Well, not you, obviously.

VERONICA. No, not me, thank God.

MICHAEL. Not you, Darjee, not you, you're a fully evolved woman, you're stain-resistant.

VERONICA. Why are you attacking me?

MICHAEL. I'm not attacking you. Quite the opposite.

VERONICA. Yes, you're attacking me, you know you are.

MICHAEL. You organized this little shindig, I just let myself be recruited …

VERONICA. You let yourself be recruited?

MICHAEL. Yes.

VERONICA. That's detestable.

MICHAEL. Not at all. You stand up for civilization, that's completely to your credit.

VERONICA. Exactly, I'm standing up for civilization! And it's lucky there are people who are prepared to do that! *(She's on the brink of tears.)* You think it's a better idea to be a fucking Neanderthal?

ALAN. Come on now, come on …

VERONICA. *(As above.)* Is it normal to criticize someone for not being a fucking Neanderthal? …

ANNETTE. No one's saying that. No one's criticizing you.

VERONICA. Yes, they are! … *(She bursts into tears.)*

ALAN. No, they're not!

VERONICA. What were we supposed to do? Sue you? Not speak to one another and try to slaughter each other with insurance claims?

MICHAEL. Stop it, Ronnie …

VERONICA. Stop what?! …

MICHAEL. You're blowing things out of proportion …

VERONICA. I don't give a shit! You force yourself to rise above petty-mindedness … and you finish up humiliated and completely on your own … *(Alan's cell phone has vibrated.)*

ALAN. … Yes … Let them prove it! … Prove it … but if you ask me, don't answer at all …

MICHAEL. We're always on our own! Everywhere! Who wants a little rum?

ALAN. … Murray, I'm in a meeting, I'll call you back from the office … *(He cuts the line.)*

VERONICA. So, you see! I'm living with someone who's totally negative.

ALAN. Who's negative?

MICHAEL. I am.

VERONICA. This was the worst idea! We should never have arranged this meeting!

MICHAEL. I told you.

VERONICA. You told me?

MICHAEL. Yes.

VERONICA. You told me you didn't want to have this meeting?!

MICHAEL. I didn't think it was a good idea.

ANNETTE. It was a good idea …

MICHAEL. Oh, please! … *(He raises the bottle of rum.)* Anybody?

VERONICA. You told me it wasn't a good idea, Michael?!

MICHAEL. Think so.

VERONICA. You think so!

ALAN. Wouldn't mind a little drop.

ANNETTE. Didn't you have to go?

ALAN. I could manage a small glass, now that we've come this far. *(Michael pours a glass for Alan.)*

VERONICA. You look me in the eye and tell me we weren't in complete agreement about this!

ANNETTE. Calm down, Veronica, calm down, this is pointless …

VERONICA. Who stopped anyone touching the clafouti this morning? Who said, let's keep the rest of the clafouti for the Raleighs?! Who said it?!

ALAN. That was nice.

MICHAEL. What's that got to do with it?

VERONICA. What do you mean, what's that got to do with it?

MICHAEL. If you invite people, you invite people.

VERONICA. You're a liar, you're a liar! He's a liar!

ALAN. You know, speaking personally, my wife had to drag me here. When you're brought up with a kind of John Wayne-ish idea of virility, you don't want to settle this kind of problem with a lot of yakking. *(Michael laughs.)*

ANNETTE. I thought your model was Spartacus.

ALAN. Same family.

MICHAEL. Analogous.

VERONICA. Analogous! Are there no lengths you won't go to to humiliate yourself, Michael?

ANNETTE. Obviously it was pointless dragging him here.

ALAN. What were you hoping for, Woof-woof? It's true, it's a ludicrous nickname. Were you hoping for a glimpse of universal harmony? This rum is terrific.

MICHAEL. It is, isn't it? English Harbor, ten years old, direct from Antigua.

VERONICA. And the tulips, whose idea was that? I said it's a shame the tulips are finished, I didn't say rush down to the Korean deli at the crack of dawn.

ANNETTE. Don't work yourself up into this state, Veronica, it's crazy.

VERONICA. The tulips were his idea! Entirely his idea! Aren't we allowed a drink?

ANNETTE. Yes, Veronica and I would like one too. By the way, it's pretty amusing, someone descended from Spartacus and John Wayne who can't even pick up a mouse.

MICHAEL. Will you SHUT UP about that hamster! Shut up! …

(He gives Annette a glass of rum.)

VERONICA. Ha, ha! You're right, it's laughable!

ANNETTE. What about her?

MICHAEL. I don't think she needs any.

VERONICA. Give me a drink, Michael.

MICHAEL. No.

VERONICA. Michael!

MICHAEL. No. *(Veronica tries to snatch the bottle out of his hands. Michael resists.)*

ANNETTE. What's the matter with you, Michael?!

MICHAEL. All right, there you are, take it. Drink, drink, who cares?

ANNETTE. Is alcohol bad for you?

VERONICA. It's wonderful. *(She slumps.)*

ALAN. Right … Well, I don't know …

VERONICA. *(To Alan.)* … Listen, Mr. Raleigh …

ANNETTE. Alan.

VERONICA. Alan, we're not exactly soulmates, you and me, but, you see, I live with a man who's decided, once and for all, that life is second-rate. It's very difficult living with a man who comforts himself with that thought, who doesn't want anything to change, who can't work up any enthusiasm about anything …

MICHAEL. He doesn't give a shit. He doesn't give a shit about any of that.

VERONICA. You have to believe … you have to believe in the possibility of improvement, don't you?

MICHAEL. He's the last person you should be telling all this.

VERONICA. I'll talk to whoever I goddamn well please! *(The telephone rings.)*

MICHAEL. Who the fuck is this now? … Yes, Mom … He's fine. I say he's fine, he's lost his teeth, but he's fine … Yes, he's in pain. He's in pain but it'll pass. Mom, I'm busy, I'll call you back.

ANNETTE. He's still in pain?

VERONICA. No.

ANNETTE. Then why worry your mother?

VERONICA. He can't help himself. He always has to worry her.

MICHAEL. Right, that's enough, Veronica! What is with this psychodrama?

ALAN. Veronica, are we ever interested in anything but ourselves? Of course we'd all like to believe in the possibility of improvement. Of which we could be the architect and which would be in no way self-serving. Does such a thing exist? In life, some people drag their feet, it's their strategy, others refuse to acknowledge the passing of time, and drive themselves demented, what difference does it make? People struggle until they're dead. Education, the miseries of the world … You're writing a book about Darfur, fine, I can understand you saying to yourself, OK, I'm going to choose a massacre, what else does history consist of, and I'm going to write about it. You do what you can to save yourself.

VERONICA. I'm not writing the book to save myself. You haven't read it, you don't know what it's about.

ALAN. It makes no difference. *(Pause.)*

VERONICA. Terrible stink of Kouros! …

MICHAEL. Terrible.

ALAN. You certainly laid it on.

ANNETTE. I'm sorry.

VERONICA. Not your fault. I was the one spraying like a lunatic … Anyway, why can't we take things more lightly, why does everything always have to be so exhausting? …

ALAN. You think too much. Women think too much.

ANNETTE. There's an original remark. I bet that's thrown you for a loop.

VERONICA. Think too much, I don't know what that means. And I don't see the point of existence without some kind of moral conception of the world.

MICHAEL. See what I have to live with?!

VERONICA. Shut up! Will you shut up! I detest this pathetic complicity! You disgust me.

MICHAEL. Come on, have a sense of humor.

VERONICA. I don't have a sense of humor. And I have no intention of acquiring one.

MICHAEL. What I always say is, marriage: the most terrible ordeal God can inflict on you.

ANNETTE. Great.

MICHAEL. Marriage, and children.

ANNETTE. There's no need for you to share your views with us, Michael. As a matter of fact, I find it slightly indecent.

VERONICA. That's not going to worry him.

MICHAEL. You mean you don't agree?

ANNETTE. These observations are beside the point. Alan, say something.

ALAN. He's entitled to his opinions.

ANNETTE. Yes, but he doesn't have to broadcast them.

ALAN. Well, yes, perhaps …

ANNETTE. We don't give a damn about their marriage. We're here to settle a problem to do with our children, we don't give a damn about their marriage.

ALAN. Yes, but …

ANNETTE. But what? What do you mean?

ALAN. There's a connection.

MICHAEL. There's a connection! Of course there's a connection!

VERONICA. There's a connection between Henry having his teeth broken and our marriage?!

MICHAEL. Obviously.

ANNETTE. We don't get it.

MICHAEL. Children consume our lives and then destroy them. Children drag us towards disaster; it's unavoidable. When you see those laughing couples casting off into the sea of matrimony, you say to yourself, they have no idea, poor things, they just have no idea, they're happy. No one tells you anything when you start out. I have an old school buddy who's just about to have a child with his new girlfriend. I said to him, a child, at our age, are you insane? The ten or twelve good years we have left before cancer or a stroke, and you're going to screw yourself up with some brat?

ANNETTE. You don't really believe what you're saying.

VERONICA. He does.

MICHAEL. Of course I believe it. Worse, even.

VERONICA. Yes.

ANNETTE. You're demeaning yourself, Michael.

MICHAEL. Is that right? Ha, ha!

ANNETTE. Stop crying, Veronica, you can see it only encourages him.

MICHAEL. *(To Alan, who's refilling his empty glass.)* Help yourself, help yourself, exceptional, isn't it?

ALAN. Exceptional.

MICHAEL. Could I offer you a cigar? …

VERONICA. No, no cigars!

ALAN. Too bad.

ANNETTE. You're not intending to smoke a cigar, Alan!

ALAN. I'll do what I like, Annette, if I feel like accepting a cigar, I'll accept a cigar. If I'm not smoking, it's because I don't want to upset Veronica, who's already completely lost it. She's right, stop sniveling, when a woman cries, a man is immediately provoked to the worst excesses. Added to which, Michael's point of view is, I'm sorry to say, entirely sound. *(His cell phone vibrates.)* … Yes, Serge … Go ahead … Put New York, the date … and the exact time …

ANNETTE. This is obscene!

ALAN. *(Moving aside and muffling his voice to escape her fury.)* … Whatever time you send it. It has to look piping-hot fresh out of the oven … No, not we're surprised. We condemn. Surprised is feeble …

ANNETTE. This goes on from morning to night, from morning to night he's glued to that cell! That cell phone makes mincemeat of our lives!

ALAN. Er … Just a minute … *(He covers the telephone.)* Annette, this is very important! …

ANNETTE. It's always very important. Anything happening somewhere else is always more important.

ALAN. *(Resuming.)* … Go ahead … Yes … Not procedure. Maneuver. A maneuver, timed for two weeks before the annual accounts, etc. …

ANNETTE. In the street, at dinner, he doesn't care where …

ALAN. … A paper in quotes! Put the word paper in quotes …

ANNETTE. I give up. Total surrender. I want to throw up again.

MICHAEL. Where's the dishpan?

VERONICA. I don't know.

ALAN. … You just have to quote me: "This is simply a disgraceful attempt to manipulate share prices … "

VERONICA. There it is. Please, help yourself.

MICHAEL. Ronnie.

VERONICA. Everything's all right. We're fully equipped.

ALAN. " … Share prices and to undermine my client," confirms Alan Raleigh, head counsel for the Verenz-Pharma company … AP, Reuters, general press, medical press, the whole nine yards … *(He hangs up.)*

VERONICA. She wants to throw up again.

ALAN. What's the matter with you?

ANNETTE. I'm touched by your concern.

ALAN. It's upsetting me!

ANNETTE. I am sorry. I must have misunderstood.

ALAN. Oh, Annette, please! Let's not us start now! Just because they're fighting, just because their marriage is fucked, doesn't mean we have to compete!

VERONICA. What right do you have to say our marriage is fucked? Who gave you permission? *(Alan's cell phone vibrates.)*

ALAN. … They just read it to me. We're sending it to you, Murray … Manipulation, manipulate share prices. It's on its way. *(He hangs up.)* … Wasn't me who said it, it was Frank.

VERONICA. Michael.

ALAN. Michael, sorry.

VERONICA. I forbid you to stand in any kind of judgment over our relationship.

ALAN. Then don't stand in judgment over my son.

VERONICA. That's got nothing to do with it! Your son injured ours!

ALAN. They're young, they're kids, kids have always given each other a good beating during recess. It's a law of life.

VERONICA. No, no, it isn't!

ALAN. Of course it is. You have to go through a kind of apprenticeship before violence gives way to what's right. Originally, let me remind you, might was right.

VERONICA. Possibly in prehistoric times. Not in our society.

ALAN. Our society? Explain our society.

VERONICA. You're exhausting me, these conversations are exhausting.

ALAN. You see, Veronica, I believe in the god of carnage. He has ruled, uninterruptedly, since the dawn of time. You're interested in Africa, aren't you? … *(To Annette, who retches.)* Feeling bad?

ANNETTE. Don't worry about me.

ALAN. I am worried.

ANNETTE. Everything's fine.

ALAN. As a matter of fact, I just came back from the Congo. Over there, little boys are taught to kill when they're eight years old. During their childhood, they may kill hundreds of people, with a machete, with a Kalash, with a thump gun, so you'll understand that when my son picks up a bamboo rod, hits his playmate and breaks a tooth, or even two, in Cobble Hill Park, I'm likely to be less susceptible than you are to horror and indignation.

VERONICA. You're wrong.

ANNETTE. *(Mocking.)* A thump gun! …

ALAN. Yes, that's what they call a grenade launcher. *(Annette spits in the basin.)*

MICHAEL. Are you all right?

ANNETTE. … Perfectly.

ALAN. What's the matter with you? What's the matter with her?

ANNETTE. It's just bile! It's nothing!

VERONICA. Don't lecture me about Africa. I know all about Africa's martyrdom, I've been steeped in it for months …

ALAN. I don't doubt it. Anyway, the ICC has already conducted an inquiry on Darfur.

VERONICA. You think I don't know about that?

MICHAEL. Don't get her started on that! For God's sake! *(Veronica throws herself at her husband and hits him several times, with an uncontrolled and irrational desperation. Alan pulls her off him.)*

ALAN. You know what, I'm starting to like you!

VERONICA. Well, I don't like you!

MICHAEL. She's a supporter of peace and stability in the world.

VERONICA. Shut up! We're living in America. We're not living in Kinshasa! We're living in America according to the principles of Western society. What goes on in Cobble Hill Park reflects the values of Western society! Of which, if it's all the same to you, I am happy to be a member.

MICHAEL. Beating up on your husband is one of those principles, is it?

VERONICA. Michael, this is going to end badly.

ALAN. She threw herself on you in such a frenzy. If I were you I'd be flattered.

VERONICA. I'll do it again in a minute.

ANNETTE. He's making fun of you, do you realize that?

VERONICA. I don't give a shit.

ALAN. I'm not making fun. On the contrary. Morality decrees we should control our impulses, but sometimes it's good not to control them. You don't want to be singing *Ave Maria* when you're fucking. Where can you find this rum?

MICHAEL. That vintage, I doubt you can.

ANNETTE. Thump gun! Ha, ha! …

VERONICA. *(Same tone.)* Thump gun, you're right!

ALAN. That's right. Thump gun.

ANNETTE. Why don't you just say grenade launcher?

ALAN. Because thump gun is correct. It's like you say Kalash instead of Kalashnikov.

ANNETTE. Who's this "you"?

ALAN. That's enough, Annette. That's enough.

ANNETTE. The great warriors, like my husband, you have to give them some leeway, they have trouble working up an interest in local events.

ALAN. True.

VERONICA. I don't see why. I don't see why. We're citizens of the world. I don't see why we should give up the struggle just because it's in our own backyard.

MICHAEL. Oh, Ronnie! Do stop shoving these thoughts for the day down our throat.

VERONICA. I'm going to kill him. *(Alan's cell phone has vibrated.)*

ALAN. ... Yes, all right, take out regrettable ... Crude. A crude attempt to ... That's it ...

VERONICA. You're right, this is excruciating!

ALAN. ... Otherwise he approves the rest? ... Fine, fine. Very good. *(He hangs up.)* ... What were we saying? ... Thump gun?

VERONICA. I was saying, whether my husband likes it or not, that no one place is more important than another when it comes to exercising vigilance.

ALAN. Vigilance ... well ... Annette, it's ridiculous to drink, the state you're in.

ANNETTE. What state? On the contrary.

ALAN. Vigilance, it's an interesting idea ... *(His cell phone.)* Yes, no, no interviews before the circulation of the press release.

VERONICA. That's it, I insist you break off this horrendous conversation!

ALAN. ... Absolutely not ... the shareholders won't give a fuck ... remind him, the shareholder is king ... *(Annette launches herself at Alan, snatches the cell phone and, after a brief look around to see where she can put it, shoves it into the vase of tulips.)* Annette, what the...!

ANNETTE. So there.

VERONICA. Ha, ha! Well done!

MICHAEL. *(Horrified.)* Oh, my God!

ALAN. Are you completely insane? Fuck!!! *(He rushes towards the vase, but Michael, who has got in ahead of him, fishes out the dripping object.)*

MICHAEL. The hair dryer! Where's the hair dryer? *(He finds it and turns it on at once, directing it towards the cell phone.)*

ALAN. You need to be locked up, you poor thing! This is incomprehensible! ... I had everything in there! ... It's brand new, it took me hours to set up!

MICHAEL. *(To Annette; above the infernal din of the hair dryer.)* Really, I don't understand you. That was completely irresponsible.

ALAN. Everything's in there, my whole life …

ANNETTE. His whole life! …

MICHAEL. *(Still fighting the noise.)* Hang on, we might be able to fix it …

ALAN. Forget it! It's fucked! …

MICHAEL. We'll take out the battery and the SIM card. Can you open it? *(Alan tries to open it with no conviction.)*

ALAN. I don't know how, I just got it.

MICHAEL. Give it to me.

ALAN. It's fucked … And they think it's funny, they think it's funny! …

MICHAEL. *(Opening it easily.)* There we are. *(He goes back on the offensive with the hair dryer, having laid out the various parts.)* You, Veronica, you at least could have the manners not to laugh at this!

VERONICA. *(Laughing heartily.)* My husband will have spent his entire afternoon blow-drying!

ANNETTE. Ha, ha, ha! *(Annette makes no bones about helping herself to more rum. Michael, immune to finding any of this amusing, keeps busy, concentrating intently. For a moment, there's only the sound of the hair dryer. Alan has slumped.)*

ALAN. Leave it, pal. Leave it. There's nothing you can do. *(Michael finally switches off the hair dryer.)*

MICHAEL. We'll have to wait a minute … *(Pause.)* You want to use our phone? *(Alan gestures that he doesn't and that he couldn't care less.)* I have to say …

ANNETTE. Yes, what is it you have to say, Michael?

MICHAEL. No … I really can't think what to say.

ANNETTE. Well, if you ask me, everyone's feeling fine. If you ask me, everyone's feeling better. *(Pause.)* … Everyone's much calmer, don't you think? … Men are so wedded to their gadgets … It belittles them … It takes away all their authority … A man needs to keep his hands free … if you ask me. Even an attaché case is enough to put me off. There was a man, once, I found really attractive, then I saw him with a square shoulder-bag, a man's shoulder bag, but that was it. There's nothing worse than a shoulder bag. Although there's also nothing worse than a cell phone. A man ought to give the impression that he's alone … if you ask me. I mean, that he's capable of being alone…! I also have a John Wayne-ish idea of virility. And what was it he had? A Colt .45. A device for creating a vacuum … A man who can't give the impression that he's a loner has no texture … So, Michael, are you happy? It is somewhat fractured, our little … What was it you said? … I've forgotten the word … but in the end … everyone's feeling more or less all right … if you ask me.

MICHAEL. I should probably warn you, rum drives you crazy.

ANNETTE. I've never felt more normal.

MICHAEL. Right.

ANNETTE. I'm starting to feel rather pleasantly serene.

VERONICA. Ha, ha! That's wonderful! … Rather pleasantly serene.

MICHAEL. As for you, Darjeeling, I don't see what's to be gained by getting publicly smashed.

VERONICA. Kiss my ass. *(Michael goes to fetch the cigar box.)*

MICHAEL. Take one, Alan. Relax.

VERONICA. Cigars are not smoked in this house!

MICHAEL. These are Cuban, Cohiba, Monte Cristo number three and number four.

VERONICA. You don't smoke in a house with an asthmatic child!

ANNETTE. Who's asthmatic?

VERONICA. Our son.

MICHAEL. Didn't stop you buying a fucking hamster.

ANNETTE. It's true, if somebody has asthma, keeping animals isn't recommended.

MICHAEL. Completely unrecommended!

ANNETTE. Even a goldfish can be risky.

VERONICA. Do I have to listen to this fatuous nonsense? *(She snatches the cigar box out of Michael's hands and slams it shut brutally.)* I'm sorry, no doubt I'm the only one of us not feeling rather pleasantly serene. In fact, I've never been so unhappy. I think this is the unhappiest day of my life.

MICHAEL. Drinking always makes you unhappy.

VERONICA. Michael, every word that comes out of your mouth is destroying me. I don't drink. I drank a mouthful of this shitty rum you're waving about as if you were showing the congregation the Shroud of Turin, I don't drink and I bitterly regret it, it'd be a relief to be able to take refuge in a little drop at every minor setback.

ANNETTE. My husband's unhappy as well. Look at him. Slumped. He looks as if someone's left him by the side of the road. I think it's the unhappiest day of his life too.

ALAN. Yes.

ANNETTE. I'm so sorry, Woof-woof. *(Michael starts up the hair dryer again, directing it at the various parts of the cell phone.)*

VERONICA. Will you turn off the blow-dryer! That thing is toast. *(The telephone rings.)*

MICHAEL. Yes! Because it could kill you! That medication is poison! Someone's going to explain it to you ... *(He hands the receiver to Alan.)* Tell her.

ALAN. Tell her what? ...

MICHAEL. Everything you know about that crap you're peddling.

ALAN. ... How are you, ma'am? ...

ANNETTE. What can he tell her? He doesn't know the first thing about it!

ALAN. ... Yes ... And does it hurt? ... Of course. Well, the operation will fix that ... And the other leg, I see. No, no, I'm not an orthopedic surgeon ... *(Aside.)* She keeps calling me "doctor" ...

ANNETTE. Doctor, this is grotesque, hang up!

ALAN. But you ... I mean to say, you're not having any problems with your balance? ... Oh, no. Not at all. Not at all. Don't listen to any of that. All the same, it'd probably be a good idea to stop taking it for the time being. Until ... until you've had a chance to get comfortably through your operation ... Yes, you sound as if you're in very good shape ... *(Michael snatches the receiver from him.)*

MICHAEL. All right, Mom, is that clear, stop taking the medication, why do you always have to argue, stop taking it, do what you're told, I'll call you back ... Lots of love, love from us all. *(He hangs up.)* She's killing me. One pain in the balls after another!

ANNETTE. Right then, what have we decided? Shall I come back this evening with Benjamin? No one seems to give a rat's ass anymore. All the same, I should point out, that's what we're here for.

VERONICA. Now I'm starting to feel nauseous. Where's the pan? *(Michael takes the bottle of rum out of Annette's reach.)*

MICHAEL. That's enough.

ANNETTE. In my mind, there are wrongs on both sides. That's it. Wrongs on both sides.

VERONICA. Are you serious?

ANNETTE. What?

VERONICA. Are you aware of what you're saying?

ANNETTE. I am. Yes.

VERONICA. Our son Henry, to whom I was obliged to give two Extra-Strength Tylenol last night, is in the wrong?

ANNETTE. He's not necessarily innocent.

VERONICA. Fuck off! I've had quite enough of you. *(She grabs Annette's handbag and hurls it towards the door.)* Fuck off!

ANNETTE. My purse! … *(Like a little girl.)* Alan! …

MICHAEL. What's going on? They've lost their shit.

ANNETTE. *(Gathering up her scattered possessions.)* Alan, help! …

VERONICA. "Alan, help!"

ANNETTE. Shut up! … She's broken my compact! And my spray bottle! *(To Alan.)* Defend me, why aren't you defending me? …

ALAN. We're going. *(He prepares to gather up the parts of his cell phone.)*

VERONICA. It's not as if I'm strangling her!

ANNETTE. What have I done to you?

VERONICA. There are not wrongs on both sides! Don't mix up the victims and the executioners!

ANNETTE. Executioners!

MICHAEL. You're so full of shit, Veronica, all this simplistic baloney, we're up to here with it!

VERONICA. I stand by everything I've said.

MICHAEL. Yes, yes, you stand by what you've said, you stand by what you've said, your infatuation for a bunch of Sudanese coons is bleeding into everything now.

VERONICA. I'm appalled. Why are you choosing to show yourself in this horrible light?

MICHAEL. Because I feel like it. I feel like showing myself in a horrible light.

VERONICA. One day you may understand the extreme gravity of what's going on in that part of the world and you'll be ashamed of this inertia and your repulsive nihilism.

MICHAEL. You're just wonderful, Darjeeling, you're the best of us all!

VERONICA. I am. Yes.

ANNETTE. Let's get out of here, Alan, these people are monsters! *(She drains her glass and goes to pick up the bottle.)*

ALAN. *(Preventing her.)* … Stop it, Annette.

ANNETTE. No, I want to drink some more, I want to get bombed out of my mind, this bitch hurls my purse across the room and no one bats an eye, I want to get drunk!

ALAN. You already are.

ANNETTE. Why are you letting them call my son an executioner?

You come to their house to settle things and you get insulted and bullied and lectured on how to be a good citizen of the planet. Our son did well to clout yours and I wipe my ass with your bill of rights!

MICHAEL. A mouthful of rum and bam, the real face appears.

VERONICA. I told you! Didn't I tell you?

ALAN. What did you tell him?

VERONICA. That she was a phony. This woman is a phony. I'm sorry.

ANNETTE. *(Upset.)* Ha, ha, ha! ...

ALAN. When did you tell him?

VERONICA. When you were in the bathroom.

ALAN. You'd known her for fifteen minutes, but you could tell she was a phony.

VERONICA. It's the kind of thing I pick up on right away.

MICHAEL. It's true.

VERONICA. I have an instinct for that kind of thing.

ALAN. And phony, what does that mean?

ANNETTE. I don't want to hear any more! Why are you putting me through this, Alan?

ALAN. Calm down, Woof-woof.

VERONICA. She's someone who tries to smooth the rough edges. Period. She doesn't care any more than you do. She's all front.

MICHAEL. It's true.

ALAN. It's true.

VERONICA. It's true! Are you saying it's true?

MICHAEL. They don't give a fuck! They haven't given a fuck since the start, it's obvious! Her too, you're right!

ALAN. And you do, I suppose? *(To Annette.)* Let me say something, honey. Explain to me in what way you care, Michael. What does the word mean in the first place? You're far more authentic when you're showing yourself in a horrible light. To tell you the truth, no one in this room cares, except for Veronica, whose integrity, it has to be said, must be acknowledged.

VERONICA. Don't acknowledge me! Don't acknowledge me!

ANNETTE. I care. I absolutely care.

ALAN. We only care about our own feelings, Annette, we're not social crusaders. *(To Veronica.)* I saw your friend Jane Fonda on TV the other day, I was inches away from joining the KKK ...

VERONICA. What do you mean, "my friend"? What's Jane Fonda got to do with all this? ...

ALAN. You're the same breed. You're part of the same category of woman, committed, problem-solving, that's not what we like about women, what we like about women is sensuality, wildness, hormones. Women who make a song and dance about their intuition, women who are custodians of the world depress us, even him, poor Michael, your husband, he's depressed …

MICHAEL. Don't speak for me!

VERONICA. Who gives a flying fuck what you like about women? Where does this lecture come from? A man like you, who could begin to give a fuck for your opinion?

ALAN. She's yelling. She's yelling like a stuck pig.

VERONICA. What about her, doesn't she yell?! When she said that little bastard had done well to clout our son?

ANNETTE. Yes, he did do well! At least he's not a sniveling little faggot!

VERONICA. Yours is a snitch, is that any better?

ANNETTE. Alan, let's go! What are we doing, staying in this dump? *(She makes to leave, then returns towards the tulips, which she lashes out at violently. Flowers fly, disintegrate and scatter all over the place.)* There, there, that's what I think of your pathetic flowers, your hideous tulips! … Ha, ha, ha! *(She bursts into tears.)* … It's the worst day of my life as well. *(Silence. A long stunned pause. Michael picks something up off the floor.)*

MICHAEL. *(To Annette.)* This yours? *(Annette takes a spectacle-case, opens it and takes out a pair of glasses.)*

ANNETTE. Thanks …

MICHAEL. Not broken? …

ANNETTE. No … *(Pause.)*

MICHAEL. What I always say is … *(Alan starts gathering up the stems and petals.)* Leave it.

ALAN. No … *(The telephone rings. After some hesitation, Veronica picks up the receiver.)*

VERONICA. Yes, darling … Oh, good … Will you be able to do your homework at Annabelle's? … No, no, darling, we haven't found her … Yes, I went all the way to the grocery store. But you know, my love, Nibbles is very resourceful, I think you have to have faith in her. You think she was happy in a cage? … Daddy's very sad, he didn't mean to upset you … Yes, you will, of course you'll speak to him again. Listen, darling, we're worried enough already about your brother … She'll eat … she'll eat leaves … acorns, horse chestnuts ... she'll find things, she knows what food she needs ... worms, snails, stuff that drops out of trash cans, she's like us, she's omnivorous ... See you soon, sweetheart. *(Pause.)*

MICHAEL. Chances are that creature's probably stuffing its face as we speak.

VERONICA. No. *(Silence.)*

MICHAEL. What do we know?

End of Play

PROPERTY LIST

Paper, pen
Art books
Cell phone
Newspaper
Tray with drinks, clafouti, plates, forks, etc.
Coffee
Coke
Basins, cloth, sponge
Perfume bottle
Hair dryer
Bottle of rum, glasses
Cigar box
Purse with compact, spectacle case with glasses

SOUND EFFECTS

Hair dryer
Phone rings

NOTES

(Use this space to make notes for your production)

NOTES
(Use this space to make notes for your production)

NOTES

(Use this space to make notes for your production)